IRIS

The views and opinions expressed in this book
are solely those of the author and do not reflect the
views or opinions of Gatekeeper Press. Gatekeeper
Press is not to be held responsible for and expressly
disclaims responsibility for the content herein.

Iris

Published by Gatekeeper Press
7853 Gunn Hwy, Suite 209
Tampa, FL 33626
www.GatekeeperPress.com

Copyright © 2023 by Ani Jones
All rights reserved. Neither this book, nor any parts
within it may be sold or reproduced in any form or
by any electronic or mechanical means, including
information storage and retrieval systems,
without permission in writing from the author.
The only exception is by a reviewer, who may quote
short excerpts in a review.

The cover design, interior formatting, typesetting, and
editorial work for this book are entirely the product of
the author. Gatekeeper Press did not participate in and
is not responsible for any aspect of these elements.

ISBN (paperback): 9781662941641

IRIS

ANI JONES

gatekeeper press
Tampa, Florida

The exploration of myself will be my life's work. Work that will never be complete. Work that will always exist in the air between the cliff's edge and the valley's belly. Briefly will it rest here, within your hands.

Contents

I live outside..1
I'm thinking about you...................................4
Without form..6
February arrives outside in mourning 8
My first girlfriend was in love with her ex, but that didn't bother me; I liked the way she kissed me.......11
She must know..12
The brain is a busy and unfurled mouth...............15
My body was not upset with me when
I let go of gender...17
I met June in the middle of April and
we painted each other................................22
You left a box of neckties...........................23
Poetry found me..29

I live outside

My home is painted in bright blues and greens
which attract butterflies into the bird's nest
the windows are doors and
the sun rises in the west and
the backyard has a front porch and my
picket fence is pink and curvy
it reminds me of my pink
                   my curvy

trees grow inside the house and
bed frames sleep outside where the stars
glow in the dark on the ceiling
I have a garden in the attic abundant with fruit
my labor is fiction
I am not
perceived here
I exist and
       exist again

I bathe in light and white lilies
surrounded by altocumulus paint and
colorful space
                      I step through
passing orange cats who bring
small acorns to my feet then
crunch on water in the plates
I set out for them
we have never asked one another for these things
though I blush every time
at the thought of them holding
their thought of me
carrying it through the wild places they wander to

IRIS

the moon hangs from the old moss trees
like a disco ball
               reflecting
off the blades of grass who sing
their favorite songs to the ladybugs
that crawl across them
after a long day of rest
they rest some more
as we all should
I have no mirrors
except the pond
my only real reflection
lies in the eyes
of my Mother
               my Nature

oh,
               how I love
                     living
                        outside

I'm thinking about you

Under the pulsing pink lights of the dive bar
Judy's house, just past midnight, you lower
to your knees
your gaze holding tightly to mine,
illuminated by the mirrorball moon,
your hand paints a line
from my hip and
                lower
to my thigh and
                further
you tattoo me
with your steady hand, the ink
                dripping
onto the floor

IRIS

melding with spilled tequila and tension
my hands are intrigued travelers
    gliding slowly
my fingers discover your lips
smiling under my palm
your eyelashes flutter like wispy butterflies
landing on my fingertips
the glass walls echo back an illusion
there are six of us
all desperate for the taste

Without form

I do not exist in any form
nor figure
I am an unspecific
unidentified glob
a gooey sort of unfamiliar
a slimy thing you
are unable to hold
lumpy space, pink and purple
a swirly idea
of self and
what it could be

IRIS

nebulous and attractive
you can't pin down
why you desire such nothing
which one day decided to be everything
which you decided to be everything as well
a mutual adoration for the scientific discovery
of my, and I, and the it of it all
whatever "it"
may or may not be

February arrives outside in mourning

Our yard
once a buzzing orchestra
is now a vacant stage
awaiting the next act
our flowers shrivel out
of tune yet, I find
temperature sitting higher
in tree branches
humming melodies
spreading lyrics
beneath our feet
we take off our socks
to feel the music
swell between our toes
there is still a song in you,
                         Perennial
you will sing again

IRIS

hymns for my father's hands who planted you
creased palms
gentle with your stem
do you remember him,
                        Perennial?
he is with your roots now
                        extending   out
can you feel him,
                        Perennial?
will he return with you in the springtime?
you rest for a while
before blooming again and
I wonder if I am mirroring you
if this lifetime of mine is
in the grand scheme of things
one short winter and
perhaps

at the end of my winter
when I sink down into the root system
I will arrive in March or April
and see him
waiting for me
in full bloom

IRIS

My first girlfriend was in love with her ex, but that didn't bother me; I liked the way she kissed me

      post soccer practice / shower steam sticking / shifting under her comforter / new aloe aftershave / a clean tank top / iced green papaya tea / black racerback binder / cologne on a soft figure / hand on a sweaty thigh / dipping one toe into the bed / dipping the whole body / submerging into her / sweet hibiscus / a consensual summer afternoon / kissing messily / with tongue / without performance / with your t shirt on / into the evening

      your former friend group / now hers / knocks at the door / the house is hers for the night / I thank her parents for saying I do / on a hot June afternoon / we drive / with fake ids / to dollar general / for a pack of smirnoff ice / sour candy / sweet lip balm / s'mores supplies / bring it all back / to her house / to this evening / to sneaking in / tipsy and kissing / on the couch / in the finished basement / we fall asleep there / in love / or something / she whispers / in my ear / about you

She must know
after Irare Sabasu

And there
you are
loving more
each day of
your lives, you mirror us
living lesbians, living out
of frames, we see reflections of ourselves there
surrounding a hand built table, we let
our partner kiss us in front of them
though we are in another lifetime, we know
you watch us, you see all that
we have blossomed into, not just I, nor you, *We*
have resisted, built our own homes, homes who are
present with us, making eye contact here
you whisper to us through the frame, *let*
your lover kiss you in the art museum, the

IRIS

coffee shop, the crosswalk, and the next
people need to witness your She-Generation
they need to see how we share
how we arrive at the same place, how we compile
into something more than ourselves, more than the
faint lines on our foreheads, the visual
on the magazine cover you see of our people dying,
we are more, we are the
past, present, and future, *touch us,* we are tangible
our skin won't burn you in the
church, we play the audio
another song by Tracy, please!
talkin' bout a revolution! replay it, please!
we spin the volume dial and let

our songs play around our hand-built table,
one after another
lyrics swell around our hand-built
community of people identifying as lesbian
who have hand-built themselves, their skin
and soul, they know
what will happen if the lesbian is liberated,
and they say, *let*
her
She must know

The brain is a busy and unfurled mouth

full of soft teeth chewing
on the idea of you
gathering notes
sandalwood, citrus
typeface, ink to the leaf
smudged by the left hand
unfamiliar to the cortex's taste buds, you
stare into the iris of possibility
your preference leaning
toward being
indigestible, confounding
identities, you prove
the flawed nature
of singularity

the human nature
of multiplicity
you are
immeasurable and
you love
every
moment
of
it

My body was not upset with me when I let go of gender

Even though they shared this fleshy home for years,
running up red stairs and
resting on the pink couch,
their goodbye was short
        complete
a kiss on the cheek,
        good luck out there

afterwards,
my body searched for the smile
stored away like a time capsule
the name
        taken
into safekeeping

only spoken by the conscious
the inner monologue
waiting
for precious earth
to embrace it
to press into
the larynx
      unpolished
sticky to the touch
humid lines
blurry curves
      but yet
here
it has been
all along

look closer
the tension braided
around my frame
unravels
    slowly
the picture is sure
    of something
the voice
    lowering
in octave
    falling
into

    now

my ears adjust
to new pronouns
which nourish like water
into the cracks
of an old cave
the broken bowl
is mending
with gold leaf and lacquer
I

       am

the
       body
I

IRIS

         am
     the
body
I
am
  the
body

I am

I met June in the middle of April and we painted each other

      laughing / without asking why / we had purple flowers / between our teeth / slicing in / two lingering herbalists / chewing on gardenias / on daydreams of each other / in thrifted denim / on hot days / under fitted caps / filled with water and wanting / to be closer / to hold the eyes a little longer / in our muddy and forgetful hands / we sit inside ephemera / eating dandelions / mending heartache / we watch bees / dance together / in the backyard / plucking chords / we both feel we've been here before / turning this corner together / again / again / again

You left a box of neckties

and I dipped my hand
into the pond of them
swimming like fish
their spotted tails spilling over
dripping cold water
onto the table
the droplets gathered together
like old friends
at the funeral
our family noticed how short
my hair was
just above
my shoulders

still enough for mom
to lean into
to play with anxiously
as more people landed
on our front steps
looking
      for you
I lost
my heart and
cut
my
hair
shorter
in need of something
          physical
to change

IRIS

to fall
      in alignment
with the intangible truth
of your absence

my neck
was exposed
to february's freezing hands
which wrapped around me
like a scarf
too small
so I went to your closet
in search of something
      more kind
something that could hold me

mom notices
tells me
I should wear your ties

   (this
   is the first time
   she has affirmed my non-
       conformity)

she must hear me
sneaking around
late at night
with masculinity

IRIS

inviting it in
playing with its hair
gazing into its eyes
in the safety
of my moonlit bedroom
bathed in starlight
in sincerity
it looks back at me
mom
    it looks back at me
she realizes
    looks back at me
realizes
    it must love me too
realizes my father
    wouldn't want me
        to go cold

ANI JONES

Poetry found me

standing outside
eyes closed
palms open
on may eleventh
rain begins
in droplets
small mirrors
on smooth olive skin
holding my face
brushing along
eyelashes like
a lover bending
time to return to me
we lay together
in fresh water
sweet blue
soft as a pillow
we can rest upon

Thank you to my family, both of origin and chosen, for holding me in a time where I felt I could have floated away at any moment, and to my professors; who held every rough draft and contemplation of this work. Iris is just as much yours as it is mine. It is a celebration of us.

www.ingramcontent.com/pod-product-compliance
Lightning Source LLC
LaVergne TN
LVHW042005060526
838200LV00041B/1879